KIDS PICK
THE
FUNNIEST
POEMS

KIDS PICK THE FUNNIEST POEMS

Selected by **Bruce Lansky**

Illustrated by **Stephen Carpenter**

Meadowbrook Press

Distributed by Simon & Schuster
New York

Library of Congress Cataloging-in-Publication Data

Kids pick the funniest poems / edited by Bruce Lansky; illustrated by
   Steve Carpenter.
         p. cm.
      Includes index.
      Summary: Contents: Me. —Parents.—Brothers and sisters.
   —Friends.—School days.—Disasters.—Monsters.—Strange stories.
   —Advice.
      ISBN 0-88166-149-X
      1. Children's poetry, American. 2. Humorous poetry, American.
   [1. Humorous poetry—Collections. 2. American poetry—Collections.]
   I. Lansky, Bruce. II. Carpenter, Steve, ill.
   PS586.3.K53 1991
   811'.07089282—dc20   91-31072
                                                          CIP
                                                           AC

Production Editor: Elizabeth H. Weiss
Keyliner: Kristi S. Kuder

Simon & Schuster Ordering # 0-671-74769-X

Published by Meadowbrook Press, 5451 Smetana Drive, Minnetonka, MN 55343.

BOOK TRADE DISTRIBUTION by Simon & Schuster, a division of Simon and Schuster, Inc.,
1230 Avenue of the Americas, New York, NY 10020.

01 02 03   17 18 19 20

Printed in the United States of America

DEDICATION

This book is dedicated to parents and teachers who want to pass on to children the joy of reading and shared laughter.

CONTENTS

Friends   33

School   43

Disasters   59

Monsters

Strange Stories

Advice

Credits
Indexes

INTRODUCTION

If you have ever read poetry to children, you know that there are a few poems they beg you to read over and over again. If you had a book of those favorite gems, you could keep your children enthralled for hours without once turning on the TV.

Unfortunately, there isn't an abundance of "read it again, please" poems. While researching this book, I read more than 300 poetry books that contained over 20,000 children's poems, and I did not find very many.

To find poems that kids love, I asked 10 elementary-school teachers in Minnesota to read poems to their students and have the children grade each poem with an A, B, C, or D. Altogether, more than 300 kids rated over 500 of the best poems I could find in order to choose the ones that we ultimately published.

It isn't surprising that kids picked poems by famous and best-selling poets like Dr. Seuss, Shel Silverstein, Judith Viorst, Jack Prelutsky, Jeff Moss, and Ogden Nash. But they also picked poems by some less famous, but equally clever, American, English, Canadian, and Australian poets whose work I discovered while traveling.

You don't have to wait for a rainy day to read these poems to your children—they won't let you wait that long! Once you've read them a few poems, they'll be hooked. And you'll be hooked, too, because your kids will think you are very, very funny, and (for a change) they won't be laughing at you, they'll be laughing with you.

Bruce Lansky

I'm Glad I'm Me

I don't understand why everyone stares
When I take off my clothes and dance down the stairs.
Or when I stick carrots in both of my ears,
Then dye my hair green and go shopping at Sears.
I just love to dress up and do goofy things.
If I were an angel, I'd tie-dye my wings!

Why can't folks accept me the way that I am?
So what if I'm different and don't act like them?
I'm not going to change and be someone I'm not.
I like who I am, and I'm all that I've got!

Phil Bolsta

Clatter

If I should list my favorite words,
They'd sound a lot like this:
Rumble, crash, snort, jangle, thump,
Roar, fizzle, splat, moo, hiss.
Not to mention gobble, clang,
Tweet, sputter, ticktock, growl;
Crackle, chirp, boom, whistle, wheeze,
Squawk, jingle, quack, thud, howl.
Then of course there's grunt, toot, cuckoo,
Thunder, bang, pop, mush,
Rattle, splash, rip, ding-dong, and . . .
My parents' favorite—*Hush!*

Joyce Armor

Things I'm Not Good At

What a shame I'm not good at making my bed
Or washing the dinner dishes.
What a pity I'm awful at broccoli-eating
And feeding my sister's fishes.
So sad I've no talent for cleaning my room,
All those jobs—it's so hard to get through them.
(If I tell you I'm no good at those kinds of things,
Maybe then you won't ask me to do them.)

Jeff Moss

Weird!

My sister Stephanie's in love.
(I thought she hated boys.)
My brother had a yard sale and
Got rid of all his toys.
My mother started jogging, and
My dad shaved off his beard.
It's spring—and everyone but me
Is acting really weird.

Judith Viorst

If I Were Ruler of the World

If I were ruler of the world,
I'd make some changes fast.
I'd say, "The ruler's always first;
His little brother's last."

The ruler's older sister
Would have to listen, too.
If I said, "Go and eat a bug,"
That's what she'd have to do.

All dinners would be different then;
You wouldn't have to finish
Peas or beans or broccoli
Or brussels sprouts or spinach.

I'd put an end to chores at home
And all that parents said.
There'd be no more: "Go clean your room!"
"Wash up!" "Go make your bed!"

My school would be all boarded up,
The classrooms still and dark.
No! Better yet—I'd knock it down
And make a brand new park!

If I were ruler of the world
Everything would be just right—
This is what I think about
As I drift off at night.

Bill Dodds

Daydream

I'd like to drill the dentist's tooth
And give the nurse a shot.
I'd like to make the grown-ups eat
The foods they'd rather not.
I'd make my teacher study math
And take a real hard test,
Then send my mother to her room
And yell, "Clean up that mess!"
And when they asked me why they're not
Allowed to just say no,
I'd put my hands upon my hips
And say, "'Cause I said so!"

Joyce Armor

whiRRRLLLLLL

Turn Off the TV!

My father gets quite mad at me;
my mother gets upset—
when they catch me watching
our new television set.

My father yells, "Turn that thing off!"
Mom says, "It's time to study."
I'd rather watch my favorite TV show
with my best buddy.

I sneak down after homework
and turn the set on low.
But when she sees me watching it,
my mother yells out, "No!"

Dad says, "If you don't turn it off,
I'll hang it from a tree!"
I rather doubt he'll do it,
'cause he watches more than me.

He watches sports all weekend,
and weekday evenings too,
while munching chips and pretzels—
the room looks like a zoo.

So if he ever got the nerve
to hang it from a tree,
he'd spend a lot of time up there—
watching it with me.

Bruce Lansky

A Sliver of Liver

Just a sliver of liver they want me to eat,
It's good for my blood, they all say;
They want me to eat just the tiniest sliver
Of yukky old slimy old slithery liver;
I'm saying no thanks, not today.

No, I'll pass for tonight but tomorrow I might
Simply *beg* for a sliver of liver;
"Give me liver!" I'll cry. "I'll have liver or die!
Oh, *please* cook me a sliver of liver!"
One piece might not do, I'll need two or a few,
I'll want tons of the wobbly stuff,
Of that quivery shivery livery pile
There may not be nearly enough.

Just a sliver, you say? No thanks, not today.
Tomorrow, I really can't say;
But today I would sooner eat slivers of glass,
Eat the tail of a skunk washed down with gas,
Eat slivers of sidewalks and slivers of swings,
Slivers and slivers of any old thing,
Than a sliver of slimy old quivery shivery
Livery liver today.

Lois Simmie

Learning

I'm learning to say thank you.
And I'm learning to say please.
And I'm learning to use Kleenex,
Not my sweater, when I sneeze.
And I'm learning not to dribble.
And I'm learning not to slurp.
And I'm learning (though it sometimes
      really hurts me)
Not to burp.
And I'm learning to chew softer
When I eat corn on the cob.
And I'm learning that it's much
Much easier to be a slob.

Judith Viorst

Who, Me?

There is a kid who lives with us
Who no one's ever seen.
He's the guy who broke our vase
And painted Fluffy green.

He drew the funny pictures
On my brother's bedroom door,
And left those worms to shrivel up
Inside my dresser drawer.
He also took my favorite cookies
From the cookie jar,
And put a tuna sandwich
In the brand new VCR.

In fact, he does most everything
That you might think is bad.
Of course he isn't really real . . .
Just don't tell Mom and Dad.

Joyce Armor

My Mother Says I'm Sickening

My mother says I'm sickening,
my mother says I'm crude,
she says this when she sees me
playing Ping-Pong with my food,
she doesn't seem to like it
when I slurp my bowl of stew,
and now she's got a list of things
she says I mustn't do—

DO NOT CATAPULT THE CARROTS!
DO NOT JUGGLE GOBS OF FAT!
DO NOT DROP THE MASHED POTATOES
ON THE GERBIL OR THE CAT!
NEVER PUNCH THE PUMPKIN PUDDING!
NEVER TUNNEL THROUGH THE BREAD!
PUT NO PEAS INTO YOUR POCKET!
PLACE NO NOODLES ON YOUR HEAD!
DO NOT SQUEEZE THE STEAMED ZUCCHINI!
DO NOT MAKE THE MELON OOZE!
NEVER STUFF VANILLA YOGURT
IN YOUR LITTLE SISTER'S SHOES!
DRAW NO FACES IN THE KETCHUP!
MAKE NO LITTLE GRAVY POOLS!

I wish my mother wouldn't make
so many useless rules.

Jack Prelutsky

Oliver's Parents in the Morning

Oliver's parents are very, very strict. This is how strict they are in the morning:

1. When Oliver's radio alarm goes off, Oliver's parents say, "Oliver, turn that rock music up as loud as it will go so it wakes the whole neighborhood! Otherwise, we will be very upset with you!"

2. At breakfast Oliver's parents say, "Oliver, you'd better make sure you spill at least *half* of those Sugar Crumblies on the floor, and don't you *dare* clean them up either!"

3. After breakfast Oliver's parents say, "Oliver, you must get dressed very, very slowly so the school bus has to honk a lot while it's waiting for you. Otherwise, you will be in deep trouble."

Oliver's parents are very, very strict. Aren't you glad they're not yours?

Jeff Moss

Oliver's Parents at Bedtime

Oliver's parents are very, very strict. This is how strict they are at bedtime:

1. At bedtime Oliver's parents won't let Oliver change into his pajamas until they have said, "Oliver, will you get into your pajamas!" at least six times.

2. After they tuck him in and say good-night, Oliver's parents won't let him go to sleep until each of them comes in from their bedroom to bring him a glass of water.

3. When they have company, Oliver's parents say, "Oliver, after we kiss you good-night, you may not go to sleep! You must get up quietly and sneak downstairs, to see what's happening at our party! Otherwise, you will be in deep trouble."

Oliver's parents are very, very strict. Aren't you glad they're not yours?

Jeff Moss

A Snake Named Rover

Mom wouldn't let me have a dog
"With all the mess they make!"
So, if I couldn't have a dog,
I said I'd like a snake.

My mother gasped quite audibly,
But Dad approved the plan.
"A snake," he gulped, "a real live snake . . .
Well, sure, I guess you can."

We went to Ralph's Repulsive Pets
And bought a yard of asp.
It coiled inside a paper bag
Held firmly in my grasp.

I put him in a big glass tank
And dubbed my new pet Rover,
But all the fun of owning it
Was very quickly over.

For all he did was flick his tongue
Once or twice each minute,
While nervous Mom rechecked the tank
To make sure he was in it.

Then one fine day, we don't know how,
My Rover disappeared.
My father told me not to fret,
But Mom was mighty scared.

We searched the house from front to back
And gave the yard a sweep.
By midnight we had given up
And tried to get some sleep.

At three A.M. my dad arose
To answer nature's call.
I heard him scream, I heard him swear,
And then I heard him fall.

For Dad had found the wayward pet
I'd given up for dead
Curled up inside his slipper,
Lying right beside his bed.

Now Rover's living back at Ralph's
With frogs, and newts, and guppies,
And now I have a dog named Spot—
She'll soon be having puppies.

Maxine Jeffris

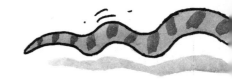

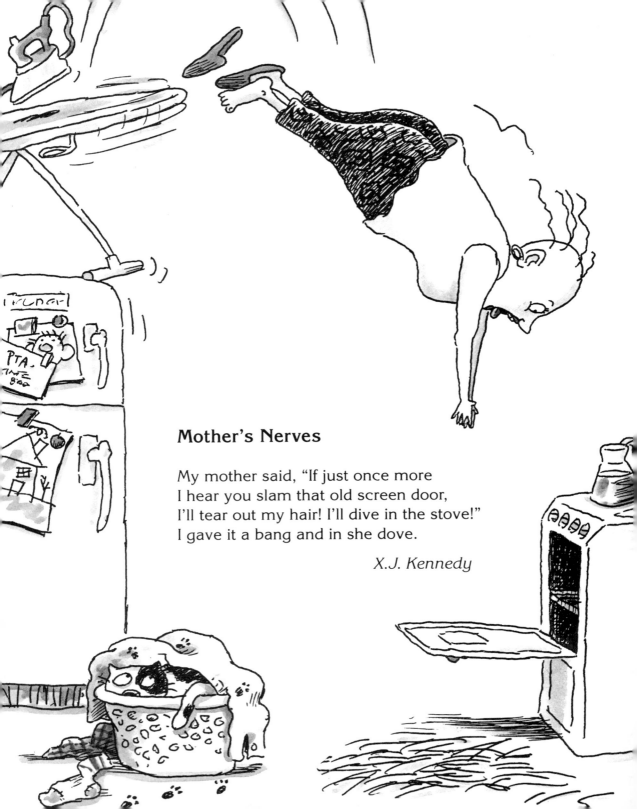

Mother's Nerves

My mother said, "If just once more
I hear you slam that old screen door,
I'll tear out my hair! I'll dive in the stove!"
I gave it a bang and in she dove.

X.J. Kennedy

BROTHERS
AND
SISTERS

My Little Sister

My little sister
Likes to eat.
But when she does
She's not too neat.
The trouble is
She doesn't know
Exactly where
The food should go!

William Wise

24

My Brother

My brother's worth about two cents,
As far as I can see.
I simply cannot understand
Why they would want a "he."

He spends a good part of his day
Asleep inside the crib,
And when he eats, he has to wear
A stupid baby bib.

He cannot walk and cannot talk
And cannot throw a ball.
In fact, he can't do anything—
He's just no fun at all.

It would have been more sensible,
As far as I can see,
Instead of getting one like him
To get one just like me.

Marci Ridlon

The Toothless Wonder

Last night when I was sound asleep,
My little brother Keith
Tiptoed into my bedroom
And pulled out all my teeth.

You'd think that I would be upset
And jump and spit and swear.
You'd think that I would tackle Keith
And pull out all his hair.

But no! I'm glad he did it.
So what if people stare.
Now, thanks to the Tooth Fairy,
I'll be a millionaire!

Phil Bolsta

The Naughty Word

My brother yelled a naughty word
When he woke up today.
He shook his crib and shouted out.
Mom asked, "What did he say?"

I looked at her and shrugged and blinked
And said I hadn't heard.
I figured I had better lie
And not repeat the word.

My brother's only twelve months old
And doesn't talk too much.
He gurgles "mama," "bye-bye," "car,"
"dada," "night-night," and such.

But now he knows another word
You don't use at the table.
You never hear it on TV
Unless your house has cable.

I've thought this through—no need to lie
Next time he drops his bomb.
I'll simply look surprised and ask,
"Just what does that mean, Mom?"

Bill Dodds

27

I Love Him Anyway

Goofball, stinkpot, pinhead, sneak,
Devil, ninny, weirdo, freak.
Crackpot, lunkhead, weasel, worm,
Donkey, lamebrain, insect, germ.
Dumb-cluck, dipstick, nitwit, dweeb,
Dingbat, bozo, fruitcake, feeb.
Moron, space-case, swine, buffoon,
Dope, chump, snake, dork, wacko, loon.
Fathead, pukeface, black sheep, skunk,
Psycho, dummy, big creep, punk.
Plus words I can't let Mother hear—
Which all describe my brother dear.

Joyce Armor

Baby Brother

He sucks and sucks
and wets his diaper,
then he grunts
and needs a wiper.

So it goes with baby brother—
in one end and out the other.

Babs Bell Hajdusiewicz

Recipe for Making Mud Pies

You need:

1 water faucet
1 garden hose
1 stick
1 backyard or flower bed

Turn on water faucet.
Grab garden hose. Push end of hose into ground to spray muddy water and pieces of grass onto clothes.
Giggle.
Repeat several times to make big puddle.
Jump up and down in puddle to mix dirt and water into mud.
Remove shoes and repeat.
Remove socks and repeat.
Use toes to mix up mud real good.
Squat down in puddle to look at mud. Make sure to get seat of pants wet.
Stir mud with stick.
Grab double handful of mud. If it stays together in a ball, it's done. If too runny, add more dirt.
Pat gently into flat shape like a pie.
Feed to little brother.

Don Stewart

30

from my
Kitchen

Sweet Dreams

It's always been a wish of mine
(Or should I say a dream)
To scare my sister half to death
And hear her piercing scream.

That's why I squished four bugs until
They all were very dead,
Then took them to my sister's room
And put them in her bed.

After we had said goodnight,
My heart began to pound.
I waited and I waited, but
She never made a sound.

And then I got so doggone tired
I couldn't stay awake.
I climbed into my own warm bed
And shrieked—there was a snake!

It wiggled, and I leaped and fell
And bruised my bottom half;
Then I heard an awful sound—
It was my sister's laugh.

Joyce Armor

Norman Norton's Nostrils

Oh, Norman Norton's nostrils
Are powerful and strong;
Hold on to your belongings
If he should come along.

And do not ever let him
Inhale with all his might,
Or else your pens and pencils
Will disappear from sight.

Right up his nose they'll vanish
Your future will be black.
Unless he gets the sneezes
You'll *never* get them back.

Colin West

Gloria

Gloria was perfect
In lots of little ways.
She had at least a million friends
And always got straight A's.
I think she was the cutest girl
That I have ever met;
The apple of her mother's eye
And every teacher's pet.

But then one day it happened.
The unthinkable, to wit:
Gloria the Perfect
Got a king-sized zit!
Big and red and puffy,
It covered half her brow.
Funny thing about it, though—
I like her better now.

Joyce Armor

The Dog

The truth I do not stretch or shove
When I state the dog is full of love.
I've also proved, by actual test,
A wet dog is the lovingest.

Ogden Nash

Willie the Burper

Some kids can talk like Donald Duck,
Some know how to chirp.
But Willie J. can swallow air
And then rip off a burp.

He'll belch at home and in the car
And at his grandma's, too.
His grandpa always laughs and says,
"That's what I used to do."

"It's not my fault," he tells his mom,
"That they're inside of me.
I feel them run around down there
And want to set them free."

It's hard to say what causes this,
But there's no use to try.
I wonder how a zillion burps
Fit in this little guy.

Bill Dodds

Suzanna Socked Me Sunday

Suzanna socked me Sunday,
she socked me Monday, too,
she also socked me Tuesday,
I was turning black and blue.

She socked me double Wednesday,
and Thursday even more,
but when she socked me Friday,
she began to get me sore.

"Enough's enough," I yelled at her,
"I hate it when you hit me!"
"Well, then I won't!" Suzanna said—
that Saturday, she bit me.

Jack Prelutsky

Could Have Been Worse

My friends have not seen London,
They've never been to France,
But yesterday at recess
They saw my underpants.

I kicked a ball, my skirt flew up
And I know what they saw.
The girls all stared and blushed and laughed,
The boys said, "Oo-la-la!"

I've thought a lot about it.
This conclusion I have drawn:
I'm embarrassed that they saw them,
But I'm glad I had them on.

Bill Dodds

The Backwards Bob Rap

Backwards Bob was a backward kid;
He said names backward—that's what he did.
Like his Aunt Pam's name, he would change
And call her Aunt Map; now isn't that strange?
He calls his Uncle Rob, Uncle Bor,
His uncle doesn't think it's funny anymore.
His little brother Drew, Bob calls Werd—
Now don't you think that's absurd?
The only names Bob leaves alone
Are Mom and Dad, and of course his own.

Larry Cohen and Steve Zweig

Katie Kissed Me

Katie kissed me!
Yuck, it's true!
My face took on a greenish hue!
My knees, like jelly, started shaking!
Then my stomach started quaking!
Slobber slithered down my cheek!
My consciousness was growing weak!
My ears were ringing, my head was spinning!
But, all the while Kate was grinning!
My heart was pounding through my shirt!
My tongue felt like I just ate dirt!
Though you may think I've lost my brain!
I wish she'd kiss me once again!

Christine Lynn Mahoney

Talented Family

My family's very talented,
I'm certain you'll agree.
We each possess a special skill
that anyone can see.

My brother's good at burying
his finger up his nose.
My sister's good at covering
her room with dirty clothes.

My father's good at eating soup
in big, disgusting slurps.
My mother's good at cutting loose
with world-record burps.

Our dog is good at piddling
in the back seat of the car.
The baby's good at putting
Pop-Tarts in the VCR.

Myself I'm good at sleeping late
and making lots of noise,
and cluttering the living room
with comic books and toys.

So though we're very talented,
I'm sad to say it's true:
We're only good at doing things
we're not supposed to do.

Kenn Nesbitt

Look Out!

The witches mumble horrid chants,
You're scolded by five thousand aunts,
   A Martian pulls a fearsome face
   And hurls you into Outer Space,
You're tied in front of whistling trains,
A tomahawk has sliced your brains,
   The tigers snarl, the giants roar,
   You're sat on by a dinosaur.
In vain you're shouting "Help" and "Stop,"
The walls are spinning like a top,
   The earth is melting in the sun
   And all the horror's just begun.
And, oh, the screams, the thumping hearts
That awful night before school starts.

Max Fatchen

... Keep your elbows off the table ...

Sick

"I cannot go to school today,"
Said little Peggy Ann McKay.
"I have the measles and the mumps,
A gash, a rash and purple bumps.
My mouth is wet, my throat is dry,
I'm going blind in my right eye.
My tonsils are as big as rocks,
I've counted sixteen chicken pox
And there's one more—that's seventeen,
And don't you think my face looks green?
My leg is cut, my eyes are blue—
It might be instamatic flu.
I cough and sneeze and gasp and choke,
I'm sure that my left leg is broke—
My hip hurts when I move my chin,
My belly button's caving in,
My back is wrenched, my ankle's sprained,
My 'pendix pains each time it rains.
My nose is cold, my toes are numb,
I have a sliver in my thumb.
My neck is stiff, my voice is weak,
I hardly whisper when I speak.
My tongue is filling up my mouth,
I think my hair is falling out.
My elbow's bent, my spine ain't straight,
My temperature is one-o-eight.
My brain is shrunk, I cannot hear,
There is a hole inside my ear.
I have a hangnail, and my heart is—what?
What's that? What's that you say?
You say today is. . . Saturday?
G'bye, I'm going out to play!"

Shel Silverstein

Michael O'Toole

Michael O'Toole hated going to school,
He wanted to stay home and play.
So he lied to his dad and said he felt bad
And stayed home from school one day.

The very next day he decided to say
That his stomach felt a bit queasy.
He groaned and he winced 'til his dad was convinced,
And he said to himself, "This is easy!"

At the end of the week, his dad kissed his cheek
And said, "Son, you've missed too much school."
"But still I feel funny, and my nose is all runny,"
Said the mischievous Michael O'Toole.

Each day he'd complain of a new ache or pain,
But his doctor could find nothing wrong.
He said it was best to let Michael rest,
Until he felt healthy and strong.

Michael O'Toole never did get to school,
So he never learned how to write—
Or to read or to spell or do anything well,
Which is sad, for he's really quite bright.

And now that he's grown, he sits home alone
'Cause there's nothing he knows how to do.
Don't be a fool and stay home from school,
Or the same thing could happen to you!

Phil Bolsta

Mrs. Stein

The school bell rings, we go inside,
Our teacher isn't there.
"Maybe she's sick!" her pet cries out.
Yeah, right. As if I'd care.

I have a D in Language Arts,
My grade in math's the same.
And now my teacher might be sick.
Could be I'm part to blame.

She doesn't like me, that's a fact,
I wouldn't tell a lie.
She says stuff like: "You're very smart,
But you don't even try."

I start to laugh—my teacher's sick!
And, boy, I'm feeling fine . . .
When someone kicks the door right in,
And there stands Frankenstein.

She's six-foot-eight, her dress is black,
She's wearing combat boots.
I start to gasp, she growls and says,
"I'll be your substitute."

The teacher's pet is whimpering;
She doesn't stand a chance.
The smart kid stares and points and faints.
The bully wets his pants.

"My name is Mrs. Stein," she says,
And every student cringes.
She leans the door against the wall,
She's knocked it off its hinges.

"Now let's begin. You there! Stand up!"
She looks me in the eye.
I try to move, my legs won't work.
I know I'm going to die!

In one big step she's next to me,
And she does more than hover.
She blocks the sun, it's dark as night,
My classmates run for cover.

"Now get up to the board," she says.
"I'd like to see some action.
Pick up the chalk, explain to us
Division of a fraction."

I leap away to save my life,
This time I *really* try.
I think and think and think and croak,
"Invert and multiply."

"Correct!" she says. I breathe again
And head back for my chair.
"You, FREEZE!" she shouts, and I stop cold.
"And don't go anywhere."

50

This all begins at nine o'clock,
I fight to stay alive.
It seems to last a million years—
The clock says nine-o-five.

That's just three hundred seconds,
And then my turn is through.
She points at every one of us—
"Now, you. Now, you. Now, you."

We all get nailed this awful day,
There's nowhere we can hide.
The lunch bell rings, we cannot eat,
We simply crawl outside.

We can't believe the other kids
Who run and play their games.
Not us, who have big Mrs. Stein—
Our world is not the same.

The bell has tolled, I must go in,
My time on earth is through.
I'll leave this on the playground—
Here's what you have to do.

You must listen to your teacher
And pray her health is fine,
Or one day soon you'll hear the words:
"My name is Mrs. Stein."

Bill Dodds

A Teacher's Lament

Don't tell me the cat ate your math sheet,
And your spelling words went down the drain,
And you couldn't decipher your homework,
Because it was soaked in the rain.

Don't tell me you slaved for hours
On the project that's due today,
And you would have had it finished
If your snake hadn't run away.

Don't tell me you lost your eraser,
And your worksheets and pencils, too,
And your papers are stuck together
With a great big glob of glue.

I'm tired of all your excuses;
They are really a terrible bore.
Besides, I forgot my own work,
At home in my study drawer.

Kalli Dakos

A Student's Prayer

Now I lay me down to rest,
I pray I pass tomorrow's test.
If I should die before I wake,
That's one less test I'll have to take.

Anonymous

My First Poem

This week at school in Language Arts,
We studied poetry.
"It's your turn now," Ms. Cratchett said,
"To write a poem for me."

So here I sit, it's after school,
I'm at the kitchen table.
I want to get this over with
As quickly as I'm able.

Now every poet uses words like
"Lo," "forsooth," "sublime."
The reason, if you ask me,
Is they need them for a rhyme.

So they come up with weird old words
That no one uses now,
That make the students cough and gag
And teachers say, "Oh, wow!"

Here's a few more antique words:
"Bemoan," "methinks," "foray."
I'm not sure what they really mean,
I think I'll get an A.

Well, that's enough, I'm done with this,
I hope you didn't choke;
This poem might be a classic
Years after we both croak.

Bill Dodds

Freddie

I don't like doing homework,
I know that it will bore me.
But now I am much happier
'Cause Freddie does it for me!

He greets me at the door each day
When I come home from school.
He just can't wait to read my books—
I think that's pretty cool!

I give him all my homework,
Like history and math.
And when he's done I give him
A nice warm bubble bath!

My grades are so much better now,
Which makes my parents glad.
Freddie is the smartest dog
That I have ever had!

Phil Bolsta

I Love to Do My Homework

I love to do my homework,
It makes me feel so good.
I love to do exactly
As my teacher says I should.

I love to do my homework,
I never miss a day.
I even love the men in white
Who are taking me away.

Anonymous

Bug

In the window of the washroom
At our school yesterday,
A little bug was crawling
In its little buggy way.

I whispered in its tiny ear
To not make any noise;
Because it was a ladybug
And the washroom is for boys.

Lois Simmie

I Found a Four-Leaf Clover

I found a four-leaf clover
and was happy with my find,
but with time to think it over,
I've entirely changed my mind.
I concealed it in my pocket,
safe inside a paper pad,
soon, much swifter than a rocket,
my good fortune turned to bad.

I smashed my fingers in a door,
I dropped a dozen eggs,
I slipped and tumbled to the floor,
a dog nipped both my legs,
my ring slid down the bathtub drain,
my pen leaked on my shirt,
I barked my shin, I missed my train,
I sat on my dessert.

I broke my brand-new glasses,
and I couldn't find my keys,
I stepped in spilled molasses,
and was stung by angry bees.
When the kitten ripped the curtain,
and the toast burst into flame,
I was absolutely certain
that the clover was to blame.

    I buried it discreetly
    in the middle of a field,
    now my luck has changed completely,
    and my wounds have almost healed.
    If I ever find another,
    I will simply let it be,
    or I'll give it to my brother—
    he deserves it more than me.

Jack Prelutsky

61

Icky

Icky, sticky, slimy sludge,
A greasy, gloppy, grimy smudge,
Oozy, swampy puddle splatter,
Gooey, gunky cookie batter.
Dirty, filthy, mucky scum,
Gluey, stringy, tacky gum,
Meat and sauce from sloppy joes—
Time, I guess, to change my clothes.

Joyce Armor

In the Motel

Bouncing! bouncing! on the beds
My brother Bob and I cracked heads—

People next door heard the crack,
Whammed on the wall, so we whammed right back.

Dad's razor caused an overload
And wow! did the TV set explode!

Someone's car backed fast and—tinkle!
In our windshield was a wrinkle.

Eight more days on the road? Hooray!
What a bang-up holiday!

X.J. Kennedy

Sarah Cynthia Sylvia Stout
Would Not Take the Garbage Out

Sarah Cynthia Sylvia Stout
Would not take the garbage out!
She'd scour the pots and scrape the pans,
Candy the yams and spice the hams,
And though her daddy would scream and shout,
She simply would not take the garbage out.
And so it piled up to the ceilings:
Coffee grounds, potato peelings,
Brown bananas, rotten peas,
Chunks of sour cottage cheese.
It filled the can, it covered the floor,
It cracked the window and blocked the door
With bacon rinds and chicken bones,
Drippy ends of ice cream cones,
Prune pits, peach pits, orange peel,
Gloppy glumps of cold oatmeal,
Pizza crusts and withered greens,
Soggy beans and tangerines,
Crusts of black burned butter toast,
Gristly bits of beefy roasts . . .
The garbage rolled on down the hall,
It raised the roof, it broke the wall . . .

Greasy napkins, cookie crumbs,
Globs of gooey bubble gum,
Cellophane from green baloney,
Rubbery blubbery macaroni,
Peanut butter, caked and dry,
Curdled milk and crusts of pie,
Moldy melons, dried-up mustard,
Eggshells mixed with lemon custard,
Cold french fries and rancid meat,
Yellow lumps of Cream of Wheat.
At last the garbage reached so high
That finally it touched the sky.
And all the neighbors moved away,
And none of her friends would come to play.
And finally Sarah Cynthia Stout said,
"OK, I'll take the garbage out!"
But then, of course, it was too late . . .
The garbage reached across the state,
From New York to the Golden Gate.
And there, in the garbage she did hate,
Poor Sarah met an awful fate,
That I cannot right now relate
Because the hour is much too late.
But children, remember Sarah Stout
And always take the garbage out!

Shel Silverstein

My Puppy Loves Flowers

My puppy's in the garden.
He loves to smell the flowers.
To help them grow my puppy always
sprinkles them with showers.

Bruce Lansky

Doing Business

My daddy's on the phone right now.
He says he's almost done.
My daddy's doing business with
a man in Washington.

My mother's doing business, too.
She's not at home today.
My mother's doing business at
her office far away.

And I'll be doing business with
our brand new pooper-scoop,
'cause my puppy's doing business on
our newly painted stoop!

Babs Bell Hajdusiewicz

67

Fifteen, Maybe Sixteen, Things to Worry About

My pants could maybe fall down when I dive off the diving board.
My nose could maybe keep growing and never quit.
Miss Brearly could ask me to spell words like *stomach* and *special.*
    (*Stumick* and *speshul?*)
I could play tag all day and always be "it."

Jay Spievack, who's fourteen feet tall, could want to fight me.
My mom and my dad—like Ted's—could want a divorce.
Miss Brearly could ask me a question about Afghanistan.
        (Who's Afghanistan?)
Somebody maybe could make me ride a horse.

My mother could maybe decide that I needed more liver.
My dad could decide that I needed less TV.
Miss Brearly could say that I have to write script and stop printing.

(i'm Better at PRINTiNG.)

Chris could decide to stop being friends with me.

The world could maybe come to an end on next Tuesday.
The ceiling could maybe come crashing on my head.
I maybe could run out of things for me to worry about.
And then I'd have to do my homework instead.

Judith Viorst

Too Many Daves

Did I ever tell you that Mrs. McCave
Had twenty-three sons and she named them all Dave?
Well, she did. And that wasn't a smart thing to do.
You see, when she wants one and calls out, "Yoo-Hoo!
Come into the house, Dave!" she doesn't get *one*.
All twenty-three Daves of hers come on the run!
This makes things quite difficult at the McCaves'
As you can imagine, with so many Daves.
And often she wishes that, when they were born,
She had named one of them Bodkin Van Horn
And one of them Hoos-Foos. And one of them Snimm.
And one of them Hot-Shot. And one Sunny Jim.
And one of them Shadrack. And one of them Blinkey.
And one of them Stuffy. And one of them Stinkey.
Another one Putt-Putt. Another one Moon Face.
Another one Marvin O'Gravel Balloon Face.
And one of them Ziggy. And one Soggy Muff.
One Buffalo Bill. And one Biffalo Buff.
And one of them Sneepy. And one Weepy Weed.
And one Paris Garters. And one Harris Tweed.
And one of them Sir Michael Charmichael Zutt
And one of them Oliver Boliver Butt
And one of them Zanzibar Buck-Buck McFate . . .
But she didn't do it. And now it's too late.

Dr. Seuss

The Creature in the Classroom

It appeared inside our classroom
at a quarter after ten,
it gobbled up the blackboard,
three erasers and a pen.
It gobbled teacher's apple
and it bopped her with the core.
"How dare you!" she responded.
"You must leave us . . . there's the door."

The Creature didn't listen
but described an arabesque
as it gobbled all her pencils,
seven notebooks and her desk.
Teacher stated very calmly,
"Sir! You simply cannot stay,
I'll report you to the principal
unless you go away!"

But the thing continued eating,
it ate paper, swallowed ink,
as it gobbled up our homework
I believe I saw it wink.
Teacher finally lost her temper.
"OUT!" she shouted at the creature.
The creature hopped beside her
and GLOPP . . . it gobbled teacher.

Jack Prelutsky

Believing

I don't believe in vampires,
I'll say it loud and clear,
I don't believe in werewolves,
when other folk are near.

I certainly don't believe in ghosts,
All those that do are fools,
And I know for an absolute positive fact,
There are no such things as ghouls.

So why, when it is late at night,
After all that I've just said,
Do vampires, werewolves, ghosts and ghouls
All gather underneath my bed?

The truth, of course, is obvious,
And plain for all to see,
For though I don't believe in *them*,
They all believe in *me!*

Willis Hall

Sock Monster

There's a thing stealing socks in our dryer, we know,
It's stealing them one by one;
It never grabs panties or stuff that won't show,
It just grabbles up socks by the ton.

I get so depressed when I start to get dressed
With that hopeless, disastrous feeling;
I'm all the time late when I can't find a mate,
Our sock pile goes up to the ceiling.

On a pretty good day there's a black and a grey
And my pants meet my shoes real nice;
When everything's right there's a cream and a white
And people don't even look twice.

If I ever find that sock-grabbing thing
It better prepare to be dead;
I'll stomp it to death with my stocking feet. . . .
A yellow one. And a red.

Lois Simmie

The Monsters in My Closet

The monsters in my closet
Like to sleep the day away.
So when I get home from school,
I let them out to play.

When Mom calls me for supper,
I give them each a broom.
First they put my toys away,
And then they clean my room.

The Mummy hates to vacuum.
So if he starts to whine,
I kick his rear and tell him,
"Trade jobs with Frankenstein."

Wolfman used to fold my clothes.
I'll give him one more chance—
Last time he wasn't careful
And left furballs in my pants.

When my room is nice and neat,
I bring them up some food.
But Dracula wants to drink my blood—
I think that's pretty rude.

When it's time to go to bed,
I hug them all goodnight.
They jump back in my closet,
While I turn out the light.

I've taken care of monsters
For as long as I recall,
But the monsters in my closet
Are the nicest ones of all!

Phil Bolsta

A Sorcerer Has Cursed Me

A sorcerer has cursed me
and I don't know what to do.
Once I had two bright blue eyes
and now I've thirty-two!

My head is pointed sharply.
I grew a three-foot nose.
My ears are like two melons.
And now I've twenty toes.

My mouth is full of long, sharp fangs.
Compared to skunks I stink.
My arms drag on the pavement.
And my hair is glowing pink!

A sorcerer has cursed me.
I must thank him right away.
For now I'm much more handsome
than I was just yesterday!

Harry Wozniak

A Strange Tale

In a cottage in Fife
Lived a man with his wife
Who, believe me, were comical folk;
For, to people's surprise,
They both saw with their eyes,
And their tongues moved whenever they spoke!
When quite fast asleep,
I've been told that to keep
Their eyes open they could not contrive;
They walked on their feet,
It was thought what they eat
Helped, with drinking, to keep them alive!
What's amazing to tell,
I have heard that their smell
Chiefly lay in a thing called their nose!
And though strange are such tales,
On their fingers they'd nails,
As well as on each of their toes!

Anonymous

Teevee

In the house
of Mr. and Mrs. Spouse
he and she
would watch teevee
and never a word
between them spoken
until the day
the set was broken.

Then "How do you do?"
said he to she,
"I don't believe
that we've met yet.
Spouse is my name.
What's yours?" he asked.

"Why, mine's the same!"
said she to he,
"Do you suppose that we could be—?"

But the set came suddenly right about,
and so they never did find out.

Eve Merriam

Help Wanted

Santa needs new reindeer.
The first bunch has grown old.
Dasher has arthritis;
Comet hates the cold.
Prancer's sick of staring
at Dancer's big behind.
Cupid married Blitzen
and Donder lost his mind.
Dancer's mad at Vixen
for stepping on his toes.
Vixen's being thrown out—
she laughed at Rudolph's nose.
If you are a reindeer
we hope you will apply.
There is just one tricky part:
You must know how to fly.

Timothy Tocher

A Social Mixer

Father said, "Heh, heh! I'll fix her!"—
Threw Mother in the concrete mixer.

She whirled about and called, "Come hither!"
It looked like fun. He jumped in with her.

Then in to join that dizzy dance
Jumped Auntie Bea and Uncle Anse.

In leaped my little sister Lena
And Chuckling Chuck, her pet hyena.

Even Granmaw Fanshaw felt a yearning
To do some high-speed overturning.

All shouted through the motor's whine,
"Aw come on in—the concrete's fine!"

I jumped in too and got all scrambly.
What a crazy mixed-up family!

X.J. Kennedy

Greedy Dog

This dog will eat anything.

Apple cores and bacon fat,
Milk you poured out for the cat.
He likes the string that ties the roast
And relishes hot buttered toast.
Hide your chocolates! He's a thief,
He'll even eat your handkerchief.
And if you don't like sudden shocks,
Carefully conceal your socks.
Leave some soup without a lid,
And you'll wish you never did.
When you think he must be full,
You find him gobbling bits of wool,
Orange peel or paper bags,
Dusters and old cleaning rags.

This dog will eat anything,
Except for mushrooms and cucumber.

Now what is wrong with those, I wonder?

James Hurley

I Saw a Jolly Hunter

I saw a jolly hunter
    With a jolly gun
Walking in the country
    In the jolly sun.

In the jolly meadow
    Sat a jolly hare.
Saw the jolly hunter.
    Took jolly care.

Hunter jolly eager—
    Sight of jolly prey.
Forgot gun pointing
    Wrong jolly way.

Jolly Hunter jolly head
    Over heels gone.
Jolly old safety catch
    Not jolly on.

Bang went the jolly gun.
    Hunter jolly dead.
Jolly hare got clean away.
    Jolly good, I said.

Charles Causley

Mr. Mixup Tells a Story

Under the rabbit there, I saw a tree—
Well, you know what I mean.
His ears were green and leafy . . . you asked me
to *tell* you, didn't you, just what I'd seen?

Well, anyhow, out peered that big red box.
Red fox? Did I say *box?* A fox it was!
He didn't see me. I looked up my clocks . . .
My *watch?* My watch to watch how long he does.

How long he *took?* A nice word, *took.* That's right . . .
to spot my rabbit up above his spine—
his pine. No, rabbits don't have wings. It's quite
enough to wiggle nose. Can't wiggle mine.

Ten days went by. You say *ten minutes?* Why?
Because it happened yesterday? It should.
Then suddenly I saw the fellow fly.
Which fellow? Couldn't he? Oh, yes, he could.

And that old boxed-up wolf. I tell you he . . .
I don't know which direction. What's the diff?
He didn't catch—he wasn't after *me.*
What rabbit? Well, speak up! No matter if.

David McCord

Eletelephony

Once there was an elephant,
Who tried to use the telephant—
No! no! I mean an elephone
Who tried to use the telephone—
(Dear me! I am not certain quite
That even now I've got it right.)

Howe'er it was, he got his trunk
Entangled in the telephunk;
The more he tried to get it free,
The louder buzzed the telephee—
(I fear I'd better drop the song
Of elephop and telephong!)

Laura E. Richards

Night, Knight

"Night, night,"
said one knight
to the other knight
the other night.
"Night, night, knight."

Anonymous

Foolish Questions

Where can a man buy a cap for his knee?
Or a key for the lock of his hair?
And can his eyes be called a school?
I would think—there are pupils there!
What jewels are found in the crown of his head,
And who walks on the bridge of his nose?
Can he use, in building the roof of his mouth,
The nails on the ends of his toes?
Can the crook of his elbow be sent to jail—
If it can, well, then, what did it do?
And how does he sharpen his shoulder blades?
I'll be hanged if I know—do you?
Can he sit in the shade of the palm of his hand,
And beat time with the drum in his ear?
Can the calf of his leg eat the corn on his toe?—

There's somethin' pretty strange around here!

American Folk Rhyme,
adapted by William Cole

A Poem on the Wrong Track

One day last winter,
A train caught cold.
It's a true story,
Or so I'm told.

For one entire month
It stood in the rain,
Coughing and sneezing,
An achoo, an achoo, an achoo choo train.

Louis Phillips

*

Once upon a time,
Can't remember when,
Way back there,
Way back then,
Someone told me something,
Can't remember who,
Can't remember what it was,
But if I ever do,
I'll write it on a thingum
And put it somewhere safe—
I think the little whatsit
Would be the perfect place.
I wouldn't trust the whoozit
With the thingamy because,
I can't remember where it is
Or where it ever was.
My memory is excellent;
It's never failed me yet.
The only things it can't recall
Are things that I forget.

Charles Wilkins

*(The author regrets that his memory
  has forgotten the title of this poem.)

91

Scrambled

I climbed up the door and
I opened the stairs.
I said my pajamas
and buttoned my prayers.

I turned off the covers
and pulled up the light.
I'm all scrambled up since
she kissed me last night.

Adapted by Bruce Lansky

92

Rules to Live By

1. Never hug a porcupine,
   or you'll get stuck with quills.
2. Never kiss a duck,
   'cause they have rough and scratchy bills
3. Never dine with pigs,
   as they can be a trifle rude.
   For they're the sort who grunt and snort
   and hate to share their food.
4. Never swim with sharks,
   or you may end up as dessert.
5. Never dress a hippo up
   in trousers and a shirt.
6. Never teach your parrot
   to sing Christmas songs in June.
7. Never let a kitten
   sharpen claws on your balloon.
8. Never let a snake
   curl up inside your mother's purse,
   or they'll be taking mom away
   inside a big black hearse.
9. Never feed an earthworm
   T-bone steak and baked potato.
10. Never let an elephant
    sit on a ripe tomato.

The Early Bird

The early bird—so I have read—
Gets the worm. I stay in bed
And put myself in the worm's shoes.
Had it stayed in for one more snooze
And then a second, then a third,
By then, would not the early bird
Have gone to feed the early cat?
I take a worm's eye view of that.
Why get up early just to start
The day as bird food? Call that smart?
Ask any worm and it will say,
"Being eaten spoils my day!"
Getting out of bed too soon
Spoils mine. Call me at noon.

John Ciardi

How I Quit Sucking My Thumb

My mother says it's childish and
my father says it's dumb—
whenever they discover that
I'm sucking on my thumb.

It's such a silly thing to do,
as everybody knows.
So now instead of sucking it
I stick it in my nose.

Bruce Lansky

Stomach Ache Supreme

If Mother asks you to make supper,
Don't protest, pout or scream.
You can use my favourite recipe
Called "Stomach Ache Supreme."

Get ice cream from the freezer,
Put it in a baking dish,
Pour some chocolate syrup on it
With a can of tuna fish.

Sprinkle it with chocolate chips,
Some salt and pepper too.
Dump a blob of honey on the top,
Now there's a "treat" for you!

Spread peanut butter on it,
Add cinnamon to taste.
Garnish it with spinach
And a jar of almond paste.

Place it in the oven
And bake it for awhile.
Then serve it to your family,
But don't forget to smile!

Give them heaping helpings,
Expect some stomach pain.
They'll never, never want you
To ever cook again!

Geraldine Nicholas

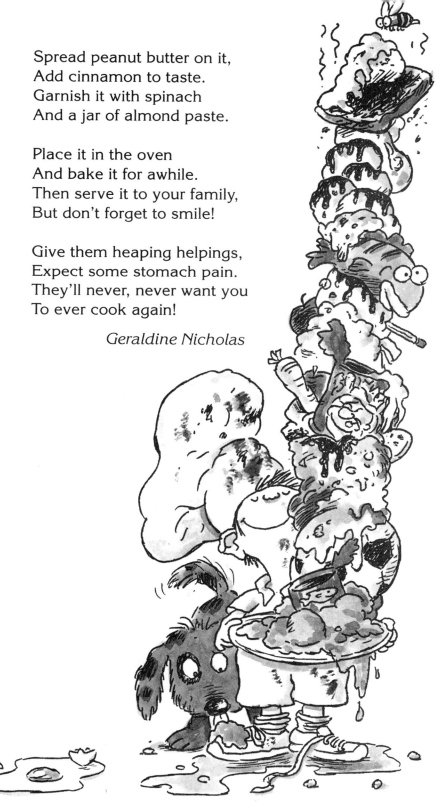

Be Glad Your Nose Is on Your Face

Be glad your nose is on your face,
not pasted on some other place,
for if it were where it is not,
you might dislike your nose a lot.

Imagine if your precious nose
were sandwiched in between your toes,
that clearly would not be a treat,
for you'd be forced to smell your feet.

Your nose would be a source of dread
were it attached atop your head,
it soon would drive you to despair,
forever tickled by your hair.

Within your ear, your nose would be
an absolute catastrophe,
for when you were obliged to sneeze,
your brain would rattle from the breeze.

Your nose, instead, through thick and thin,
remains between your eyes and chin,
not pasted on some other place—
be glad your nose is on your face!

Jack Prelutsky

Turning Off the Faucet

If you don't turn the faucet off tight
When you're done in the bathroom,
You'll be wasting water.
Also, the sink might fill up
And overflow and flood the bathroom,
And then the bathroom would fill up
And overflow and flood the bedroom,
And all your clothes would get soaking wet,
And when you wore them, you'd catch a horrible cold
And have to stay home from school
And you couldn't learn anything
Or see your friends.

And after you'd missed school long enough,
All your friends would forget you
And you would be so sad and wet
You'd probably just stay in bed
Wearing your sad, wet clothes
With your sad, wet head
On your sad, wet pillow
Until you just shrivelled up and wasted away.
And nobody would care.
Except your parents
And they'd be all sad and wet
And shrivelling and wasting away, too,
Because you didn't turn the faucet off.

Jeff Moss

How to Talk
on the
Telephone

Hello. Is your refrigerator running? Then you'd better go and catch it.

Hello. Is this the cigar store? Do you have Muriel in a box? Well, you'd better let her out before she suffocates.

Hello. Is this the drugstore? Do you have Bayer Asprin? Cover it up; it's going to catch cold.

Hello. Is this Mr. Goose? Is your mother there?

Hello. I'm taking a survey. Have you ever eaten peanut butter and amatta? What's amatta? I don't know. What's amatta with you?

Hello. Are you English? Are you Swedish? Are you Italian? Are you Finnish? Well, I am. Good-bye.

Hello. I'm taking a survey. Do you have a television? How many kids do you have? Do you eat spinach? Thank you. Good-bye.

Hello. We have a call for you from Washington. Please stand by; we'll call you back.

Hello. Are you expecting a call from Washington? Well, then you must be crazy because he's been dead for a thousand years.

Hello. Is Ralph Peterson there?
Hello. Is Ralph Peterson there?
Hello. Is Ralph Peterson there?
Hello. Is Ralph Peterson there?
Hello. Is Ralph Peterson there?
Hello. This is Ralph Peterson. Are there any messages for me?

Hello. Is this the grocery store? Do you have pig's feet? Then how do you get your shoes on in the morning?

Delia Ephron

Stop Sniffling!

If you should have the sniffles,
you'd better blow your nose.
Because if you should go "Achoo!"
you'll mess up all your clothes.

Bruce Lansky

CREDITS

The publishers have made every effort to trace ownership of the copyrighted material contained in this anthology and to secure all necessary permission to reprint. In the event that any acknowledgment has been inadvertently omitted, we express our regrets and will make all necessary corrections in future printings.

Grateful acknowledgment is made to the following for permission to reprint the copyrighted material listed below:

Joyce Armor for "Clatter," "Daydream," "Who, Me?" "I Love Him Anyway," "Sweet Dreams," "Gloria," and "Icky" by Joyce Armor. Copyright © 1991 by Joyce Armor. Used by permission of the author, Joyce Armor.

Bantam Books for "Things I'm Not Good At," "Oliver's Parents in the Morning," "Oliver's Parents at Bedtime," and "Turning Off the Faucet" from The Butterfly Jar by Jeff Moss. Copyright © 1989 by Jeff Moss. Used by permission of Bantam Books, a division of Bantam Doubleday, Dell Publishing Group, Inc.

Phil Bolsta for "I'm Glad I'm Me," "The Toothless Wonder," "Michael O'Toole," "Freddie," and "The Monsters in My Closet." Copyright © 1991 by Phil Bolsta. Used by permission of the author, Phil Bolsta.

Clerkenwell House for "Look Out!" from Songs For My Dog and Other People by Max Fatchen. Originally published by Kestrel Books, 1980. Copyright © 1980 by Max Fatchen.

Larry Cohen and Steve Zweig for "The Backwards Bob Rap." Copyright © 1991 by Larry Cohen and Steve Zweig. Used by permission of the authors, Larry Cohen and Steve Zweig.

Curtis Brown, Ltd. for "Mother's Nerves" and "A Social Mixer" from One Winter Night in August and Other Nonsense Jingles by X.J. Kennedy. Copyright © 1975 by X.J. Kennedy. "In the Motel" from The Phantom Ice-Cream Man by X.J. Kennedy. Copyright © 1979 by X.J. Kennedy. All selections reprinted by permission of Curtis Brown, Ltd.

David Higham Associates Limited for "I Saw a Jolly Hunter" from Figgie Hobbin by Charles Causley. Copyright © by Charles Causley.

Bill Dodds for "If I Were Ruler of the World," "The Naughty Word," "Willie the Burper," "Could Have Been Worse," "Mrs. Stein," and "My First Poem" by Bill Dodds. Copyright © 1991 by Bill Dodds. Used by permission of the author, Bill Dodds.

TITLE INDEX

AUTHOR INDEX

What People Say about Bruce Lansky's Poetry:

What librarians say:

"Bruce Lansky's poetry books are so funny, we can't keep them on our library shelves." —Lynette Townsend, Lomarena Elementary, Laguna Hills, California

"As soon as the library opens in the morning, there is a line of children waiting for Bruce Lansky's poetry books." —Kay Winek, Pattison Elementary, Superior, Wisconsin

What teachers say:

"Some of my students don't like reading, but once they open one of Lansky's poetry books, I can't get them to close it." —Suzanna Thompson, Holy Name Elementary, Wayzata, MN

"Bruce Lansky turns reluctant readers into avid readers."—Sharon Klein, Clardy Elementary, Kansas City, MO

"Bruce Lansky is the 'Pied Piper of Poetry.' He gets children excited about reading and writing poetry."—Mary Wong, Explorer Middle School, Phoenix, AZ

"There's no doubt about it—Bruce Lansky is the king of giggle poetry."—Jody Bolla, North Miami Elementary, Aventura, FL

What critics say:

"Guaranteed to elicit laughs when read alone or aloud to a class."—*Booklist*

"When I read any of his poems, it's giggles galore."—*Instructor* magazine

What kids say about Bruce Lansky's gigglepoetry.com:

"I really like your site. I used to hate poetry, but you guys make it fun."—Christina, Texas

"Even though I'm from outer space, I can speak and read your language. These poems are cool. On my planet, all we ever do is sit around and watch TV." —Me, Outer Space

"I really love this website. It is awesome! It gives me stuff to do when I am grounded." —Tiffany, Enid, Oklahoma

"I think these poems are the best poems ever!!! If you ever get down, they will make you feel better!!! —Hadassah, Augusta, Georgia

"My teacher wanted to read some poems. I gave her some I found on gigglepoetry.com. The whole class laughed like mad zombies." —Jolin, Singapore

Poetry Books by Bruce Lansky:

A Bad Case of the Giggles
Kids Pick the Funniest Poems
Miles of Smiles   1 3 2 0 2
Poetry Party

Happy Birthday to Me!
The New Adventures of Mother Goose
No More Homework! No More Tests!
Sweet Dreams

For information about inviting poet/author Bruce Lansky to your school or conference, or to order a free Meadowbrook Press catalog, write or call toll free:

Meadowbrook Press, 5451 Smetana Drive, Minnetonka, MN 55343, 800-338-2232
www.meadowbrookpress.com   www.gigglepoetry.com